ADVANCED LOCK PICKING SECRETS

D1789432

ADVANCED LOCK PICKING SECRETS

Steven Hampton

PALADIN PRESS
BOULDER, COLORADO

Also by Steven Hampton:

Secrets of Lock Picking
Security Systems Simplified

Advanced Lock Picking Secrets
by Steven Hampton

Copyright © 1989 by Steven Hampton
ISBN 0-87364-515-4
Printed in the United States of America

Published by Paladin Press, a division of
Paladin Enterprises, Inc., P.O. Box 1307,
Boulder, Colorado 80306, USA.
(303) 443-7250

Direct inquiries and/or orders to the above address.

PALADIN, PALADIN PRESS, and the "horse head" design
are trademarks belonging to Paladin Enterprises and
registered in United States Patent and Trademark Office.

All rights reserved. Except for use in a review, no
portion of this book may be reproduced in any form
without the express written permission of the publisher.

Neither the author nor the publisher assumes
any responsibility for the use or misuse of
information contained in this book.

Illustrations by Bill Border

Visit our Web site at www.paladin-press.com

Contents

Acknowledgments

I would like to give special thanks to several people for their assistance with the research and development of this book. Mr. Steven Hillius, EE, provided the portable magnetic lock pick circuit design. I would like to thank Mr. Craig Herrington and Mr. Jack Folkerth for their help in creating and testing the new lock pick designs. Finally, I would like to thank a very good friend and kung-fu Master, Mr. Lucjan Shila, and Sensei John Angelos, for their contribution of the "Energizing Hands" exercise.

Introduction

The art of lock picking has been a closely guarded secret for centuries. Locksmiths discuss the subject mostly with other locksmiths and require patience and devotion from those they teach. With this book, along with my previous book *Secrets of Lock Picking* (available from Paladin Press), you can learn the secrets needed to become a master lock picker at your own pace. This knowledge took me twenty-five years to discover and learn, and I hope you can benefit from it. In any case, it is important that we discuss some mental attitudes involved with having such powerful knowledge and skills.

One of the main ingredients in becoming a master lock picker is confidence. You should feel that you *can* open that lock. Have confidence that you have the background knowledge to pick locks and make your own tools, and that you have the practical experience that will make you feel comfortable around a locked door, car, or box. The nervous, excited feeling you get before you pick a lock has subsided, and opening the lock is just a matter of getting your picks out of your wallet. That kind of confidence comes from experiences which you must now have or you wouldn't be reading this book. There should be no doubt in your mind that you have the right stuff. And you do.

The second quality of a master lock picker is the ability to improvise when you are without lock picks—to be able to use such things as paper clips, small screwdrivers, pieces of wire, and hacksaw blades as tools. In other words, tools are always available to the master lock picker. And after finishing this book, you'll know, in greater detail, how to make your own professional tools.

Third, you have the understanding that if you break into a locked premise illegally, you could go to jail and not collect $200. I really did not want to write about such a negative subject, but it is important that we, as master lock pickers, have some integrity. With our knowledge and skills, we need to maintain some kind of code. For instance, I only pick locks for fun and emergencies. Being broke is not an emergency. If it comes down to it, you can probably get a job as a locksmith apprentice. If you encounter someone locked out of his house or car, and you are going to help him get in, be sure he can prove the property belongs to him. At least, ask to see his driver's license, just in case the police get involved.

So, those three qualities—confidence, skillful means of applying tools for the purpose, and caution when it comes to breaching the security of unknown situations—will keep you out of trouble and let you enjoy your skills as a master lock picker.

Another important factor to realize is that practice does make perfect. You not only project yourself into the lock you are picking, but the process of mere repetition will accumulate to make your fingers very skillful. By projection, I am referring to the intense concentration that leads to visualization of all the inner workings of the lock you are picking.

As I also mentioned in my previous book, a firm yet gentle touch on the tension wrench is needed along with a sense of *heightened sensitivity,* which is basically developed through practice and mind*full*ness – being fully aware of what one is experiencing while picking a lock. One of my favorite scenes from a popular private investigator show on television is where the star is trying to break into his house while the "lads" (two Doberman pinscher dogs) are madly racing toward him. He repeats over and over to himself, "Concentrate on the lock, don't look at the dogs, concentrate on the lock." Of course, he gets in, just in the nick of time. So, success is simply based on concentration, which develops into heightened sensitivity through practice and remembering to focus: concentration is the key.

Making the Tools

The fundamentals of lock picking were covered in my first book, *Secrets of Lock Picking*. In this volume, we will expand on tool design and manufacture, and look at the development of further skills needed to successfully pick open most locks on the market today. Security is an uncertain endeavor at best. Since there is an infinite variety of ways to secure property and valuables with locking mechanisms, it is natural that the even greater variety of ways to open locks would spawn new tools. Having the right tools is very important: good tools make difficult locks open faster and easier. The ideal tools should be durable, portable, easy to use, and effectively designed to open a lock quickly. In this book, I would like to introduce some new tools my research company has designed and tested, and also show you how to make your own. This is not as difficult as you may think since these tools are made from easily obtainable metal stock. You should be aware that these tools are not on the market; they were developed solely for myself and my advanced students.

All you need to start a lock pick factory is an inexpensive 5-inch bench grinder with cutoff wheel on one side, a pair of needle-nose vise grips, spray paint and stick glue for making the patterns, and a burnishing or Scotch-Brite wheel attachment for smoothing up rough edges.

With this simple setup and a little practice, you can create virtually any kind of lock picking tool you will ever need. You can even create your own style if you so desire. Your first few tools may not turn out as you planned, but don't be discouraged: by the second or third try, your picks will look professional. Also, you'll never be without good lock picks since you will be able to whip up a set in minutes.

The bench grinder I use is a 5-inch Black and Decker, Model 790I with a 1/2-inch arbor and 3600 RPM. This little plastic-cased grinder costs about $30 at discount stores, and I have made hundreds of lock picks with it. If you can find a reasonably priced 6-inch grinder, go for it.

Be very sure that you read and understand all of the safety rules involved with bench grinders and wear goggles or eyeglasses with safety lenses. If you have glasses made with safety glass, they may protect your eyes, but they could be damaged by burn spots. I wear high temperature plastic safety lenses, mostly because of their light weight and their resistance to burn spots. Also, don't wear polyester shirts or pants, as you could burn tiny holes in them; wear old cotton work clothes instead.

When buying a cutoff wheel and burnisher, be sure that they are rated at or over the RPM limit of your grinder. Since I am right-handed, I mounted the cutoff wheel on the right side of the grinder for easier maneuverability. Make sure that the arbor nuts are tight. The tool rest must also be level and tight. You will have to mount it on your workbench or an old table for good stability. Mine is mounted on a 2-foot by 3-foot, 1-inch thick board with 8-inch legs. With this setup, I can put it on a tabletop and stand while grinding. I also bored a 4-inch hole in front of the grinder for a water cup for quenching the metal to cool it down.

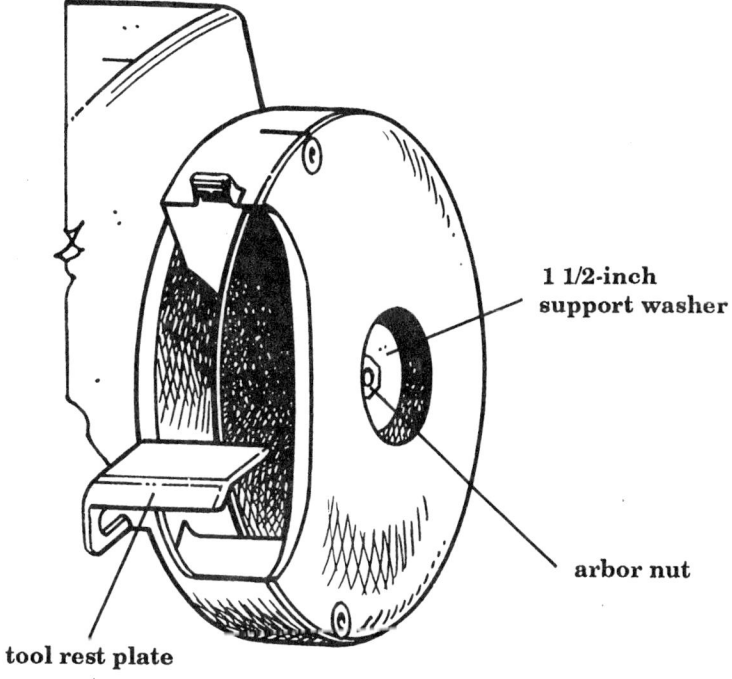

1 1/2-inch support washer

arbor nut

tool rest plate

Figure 1. Cutoff wheel.

The Basic Lock Pick Set

After years of research and practice, I have designed a set of picks that will let you into about 80 percent of the cylinder locks that you might encounter in an average day. The pick illustrated in Figure 2 is made from a flat stainless steel steak knife. Steak knives are generally .032 inch to .035 inch thick and are already hardened; used as stock, they make durable and long-lasting picks. When properly cut out with a cutoff wheel and touched up with a grinding stone, they will outlast any commercial picks. Tension wrenches are about .040 inch to .045 inch thick, and I get that stock from pancake turners, spatulas, or large bread knives.

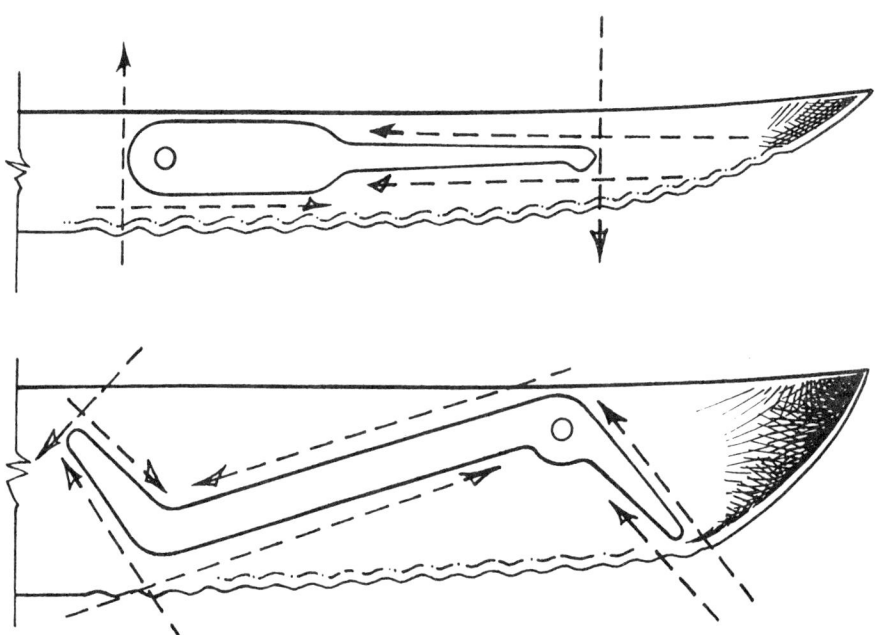

Figure 2. Lock pick tools made from steak-knife stock.

This tension wrench design allows you to open virtually all keyed tumbler locks with its long, narrow end. Automobile locks and other large tumbler locks demand the use of a wider and stiffer wrench which is on the other end of this design. The pick design is a diamond type that is medium sized to accommodate tight keyways and still have enough strength to prevent bending under normal lock-picking conditions.

All tool patterns illustrated in this book are the exact size of the tools. Make two photocopies of them to avoid destroying your book. Cut out one copy carefully, inside the line, with an X-ACTO knife. Clean the stainless steel stock with rubbing alcohol and wipe dry with a paper towel. Now, glue your pattern onto the steel, making sure that you place it exactly where you want it, without sliding it around on the stock. I use stick glue and apply it to the paper pattern only. Gently press down, without squishing glue out over the edges of the pattern. Let it dry for about ten minutes and spray paint over it with a high-temperature paint. I like a flat black paint, simply because of the greater contrast against the shiny steel, allowing one to see the pattern better. After another ten minutes, bake the painted steak knife for another twenty minutes in a warm oven at 200 degrees. When you take the painted pattern out of the oven, put it in a place where it won't be disturbed and let dry overnight.

The next day, carefully remove the painted paper pattern from your stock. You are ready to cut and grind. You can use this paper-to-steel technique with almost any lock-opening tool you want to make. If you want to duplicate a tool you have already made, just place it on your steel stock and spray paint directly over it. Let it set for sixty seconds and remove the tool from your stock by lifting it directly up with a large magnet. Be sure to hold the stock down while doing this.

When you have completed cutting and grinding your new tool, use the second photocopy to make final touchups and sizing. A finished tool should fit within the lines of the drawing.

Before you start grinding, here are a few helpful tips to make the job easier and more successful. The dashed lines with the arrows in the illustrations are the paths your cutoff wheel takes. This helps to eliminate excessive grinding. Use your vice grips to hold the stock. When that is completed, the rough form is ready to grind in smooth, even strokes. After final touch-ups are made, use a burnishing wheel to smooth out any sharp edges and corners. The burnishing wheel I use looks and feels like very hard rubber. It is impregnated with Carborundum.

If you have trouble getting the pick smoothly into a keyway of a standard pin tumbler house lock, you may have to lower the diamond point slightly by using the burnishing wheel on the bottom side of the pick's shaft only.

Also remember to quench the steel with water every three or four seconds when cutting and grinding. You don't want to void the steel's temper by getting it hot to the point of dark blue discoloration. If you can avoid the straw-yellow discoloration, do so as much as you can, but this is often not completely possible.

The holes are optional. I do this part of the job last. The holes must be drilled by a drill press with a sharp, high speed carbon drill bit about 1/8 inch in diameter. Stainless steel is very hard and dulls bits quickly. If you don't have a drill bit sharpener, plan on one drill bit per tool. They are about one dollar apiece, so this is not a major expense. Center-punch the holes before drilling, and avoid hitting the punch any harder than if you were starting a nail into wood.

Angular Pin Tumbler Locks

The Medeco Lock Company has designed a sophisticated lock which I refer to as an angular pin tumbler. Not only do the pins have to be raised to their proper shear point, they must also twist or turn in order to clear the cylinder-shell line. The pins are cut at an angle rather than on a horizontal plane. The keyway is also tightly corrugated to restrict foreign objects such as picks. Figure 3 shows a Medeco key with its angled cuts. This type of lock is considered by most locksmiths to be a high security device, and keying one up requires special tools.

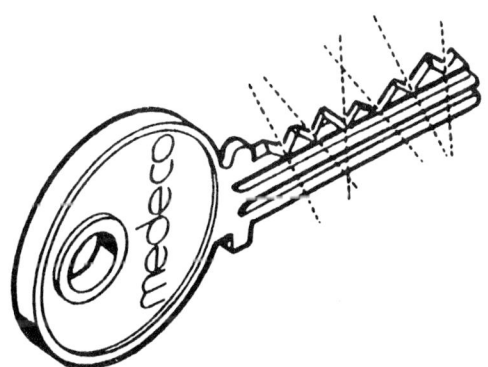

Figure 3. Medeco key.

One of the newest developments in pick design is my twisted-wedge point lock pick. It is very effective on these locks. To make this pick, take a standard diamond pick and put it in a vise with only the last 1/32 inch of the tip exposed. Heat gently with a propane torch for thirty seconds. Using a pair of pliers, gently twist the tip 15 degrees as shown in Figure 4. The vise will absorb most of the heat to keep the shaft of the pick from losing its temper. Remember to heat the tip until it turns blue, then twist. The tip will lose its temper, but it is not involved with much stress when picking so it will be all right. It is still harder than brass and will hardly wear. After it has cooled, carefully file it to a wedge-like shape, keeping the angle even. Burnish to remove any discoloration and file marks. If you have trouble getting this pick into the Medeco keyway, carefully grind off the bottom of the pick's shaft along its whole length until it slides in with little effort.

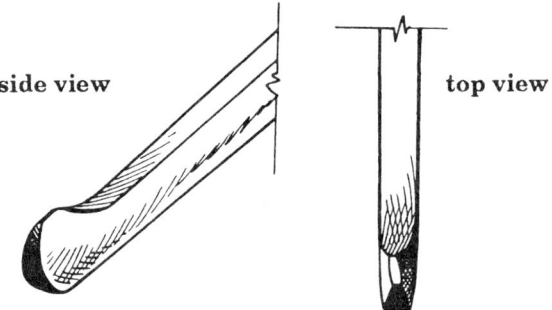

side view   top view

Figure 4. Twisted-wedge point pick.

One should practice with an old Medeco lock before attempting to open one in an emergency. The lock must be picked as if you were "raking" the tumblers so as to allow the pins to rotate as they are raised. A feather-touch tension wrench must be used. These locks require a lot of play with the tension wrench because the pins must be free to rotate. I have had much success picking these locks with the twisted-wedge point pick and a feather-touch wrench. The feather-touch wrench is used until the pins have reached their shear point and the cylinder has been freed. At that point, a standard tension wrench or small screwdriver is needed to turn the cylinder to unlock the lock.

A major drawback to these locks (along with most other pin tumbler locks), which is to your advantage, is that they are made with relatively soft brass and can be easily drilled. The cylinder can then be turned with a medium screwdriver, shearing the tumbler springs and unlocking the lock. Drill 1/16 inch above the top of the keyway about 7/8 inch into the lock. This obviously destroys the lock, which runs about $125 at 1988 prices.

Rim Cylinder Locks

There are two major manufacturers of rim cylinder locks; the two different cylinder sizes are typically classified as large and small. These locks are basically pin tumbler-type locks that have their shear lines arranged on a circular plane rather than on a horizontal one. There are usually seven pins, and each one has to be depressed a predetermined distance to its individual shear line. When all of them are at shear point, the cylinder, located at the center of the lock, can be turned, thus unlocking the lock.

The major security factor of these locks is that the pins lock up again when the cylinder has turned only 51 degrees and must be picked two to three more times in order to accomplish the desired 180 degrees to unlock the lock. This takes a lot of time and patience, which discourages illegal entry. Another factor that makes the rim cylinder lock a good security device is that it is very difficult to get a firm grip on the cylinder. Needle-nose pliers just get in the way of the pick and tumblers. Even L-shaped tension wrenches have a tendency to slip out just when the cylinder feels ready to turn.

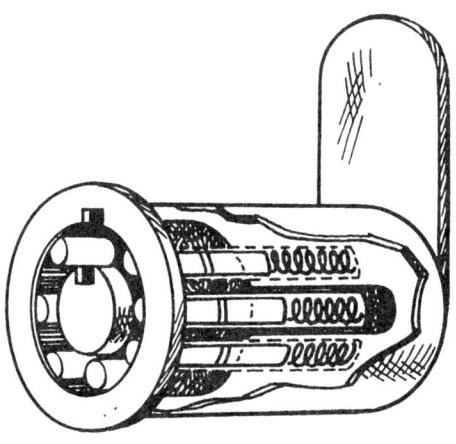

Figure 5. Rim cylinder lock.

One day while working on my plumbing, I got an idea. By designing a U-shaped tool to be used like a pipe wrench, one can grab hold of the cylinder with it and still have plenty of room for the pick to do its thing. When placed across the cylinder and used with a straight pick, this type of wrench would really speed up the process of picking these locks. The prongs of the wrench must not be burnished but left with sharp right angles for better gripping. Needless to say, it worked great. We will discuss how to make a tool that has this feature in three different sizes later in this chapter.

In an emergency, there is also the "make my day"

method in which you cut the pins out of the lock with a hole saw (without the centering drill bit). The cylinder is then turned with electrician's pliers or needle-nose vise grips.

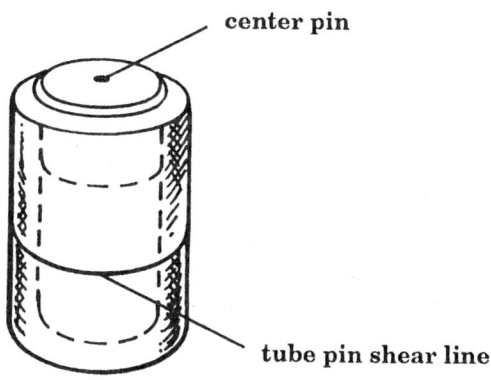

Figure 6. Lock cylinder.

Another new development in lock technology that you should be aware of are the tube pins used on the higher security rim cylinder locks. They are tube-like structures with shear lines and usually surround four of the seven pins, making for a total of eleven pins. The lock is picked the same way as a regular rim cylinder, but takes even more time to open. Once the solid pins have been set with your pick, you must go back and depress the tube pins to their shear lines.

Mushroom and Spool Pin Tumbler Locks

Spool refers to the top pins and *mushroom* refers to the bottom pin, the one that gets picked. These pins are

machined down to resemble spools and mushrooms so
as to foil any picking attempts. They are installed in

Figure 7. Spool pin (left) and mushroom pin (right).

pin tumbler locks that are used in relatively high security situations. The indication that one has encountered
a lock with these pins is that the cylinder seems to want
to turn while picking, but stops short at about 10 or 15
degrees of its turning radius. They give a false sense of

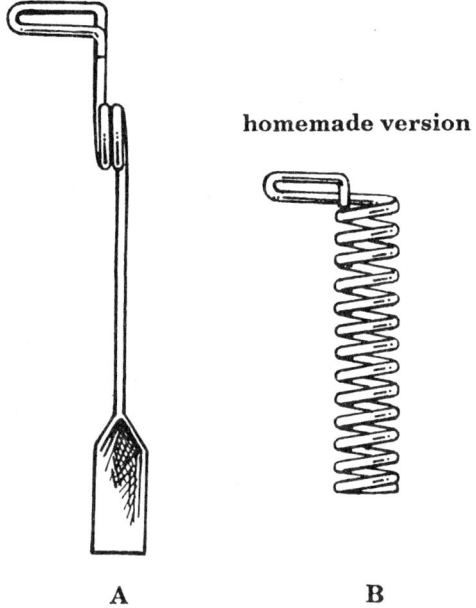

homemade version

A   B

Figure 8. Feather-touch tension wrenches.

success by giving an audible and physical sensation that the lock cylinder has been released. In reality, the cylinder has been caught in the middle of one of these pins.

This problem can be overcome by using a feather-touch tension wrench (see Figure 8A). A feather-touch wrench is a spring-loaded tension wrench that regulates a slight pressure on the cylinder, which allows you to "bounce" these pins into place at their shear points with your pick. This may appear to be a sloppy way of picking a pin tumbler lock, but it is the only way one can overcome the tendency of these pins to snag on the shear line. This is a case where being sloppy requires more skill than being skillful.

Once the cylinder has been freed, a standard tension wrench or small screwdriver must be used to turn the cylinder and operate the unlocking action of the cam. Figure 8B shows a homemade version of the feather-touch wrench made from a medium-light duty spring. A pair of needle-nose pliers is needed to bend the loop that slides into the cylinder's keyway.

These pins are used in bank door locks and in other areas that are usually backed up with burglar alarm systems. Some padlocks have these pins. The American Lock Company uses them in its stainless steel-cased padlocks, which are machined to close tolerances and can be quite a challenge to pick open. But like most other locks, they can be picked open by an experienced lock picker with the right tools.

Another mushroom pin tumbler lock is the West German-made Diskus padlock from the Abus Lock Company. It has a stainless steel case with only four tumblers and a small corrugated keyway. It sounds simple, but I've seen this little padlock put locksmiths

Figure 9. Mushroom and spool pin padlock.

into contortions to pick it open. It's hard to hang onto, even though it's over 2 1/2 inches in diameter. The cylinder is mounted upside down and the tight keyway has those four tiny pins with a mushroom cut, which makes this lock one of the hardest to pick. Part of the problem is that most conventional diamond picks are too large for the keyway. Figure 10 is a smaller version of the diamond and should only be used with locks like this one, since the pick's shank is narrower and could bend on conventional locks.

One of my lock picking successes was picking one of these open (without ever seeing one before) in front of two master locksmiths who said it couldn't be done. If you have practiced the skills covered in my first book and have read thus far into this book, chances are you would be able to open an Abus Diskus padlock. To feel the round bolt slide open on this lock is a real feeling of success, and I hope you have a chance to open one. They cost about $12. Not only can you use it for practice, it is a very good padlock for personal use.

Figure 10 shows a pattern for a small diamond pick, which is required to open locks with small, tight keyways.

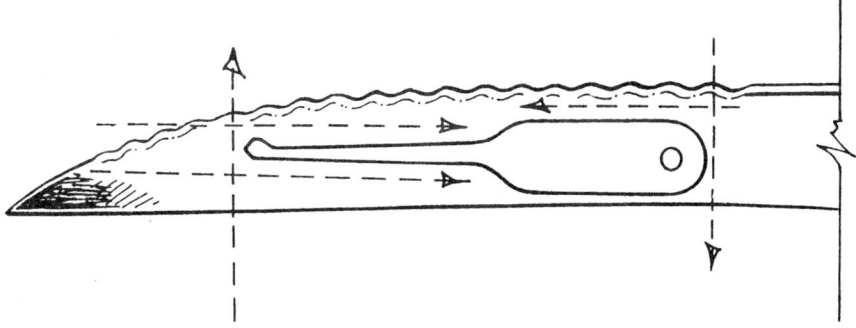

Figure 10. Small diamond pick.

Universal Tension Wrench

Since a simplistic approach to lock picking is so successful, creativity can find its outlet in the area of lock pick design. The idea would be to develop simple, yet multifunctional and easy-to-carry lock picks. Also, designing new tools is fun.

Figure 11 illustrates a tension wrench I designed and made that is very handy to have around. It is called the "Dragon." It is a universal or multiple-use wrench that is like having six different wrenches in one wallet-size tool. It features three different types of rim cylinder tension wrenches, a double wafer lock wrench, an auto lock wrench, and a long, narrow snout for virtually all types of pin and wafer tumbler locks. The "legs" of the Dragon have a pipe wrench-like gripping action on rim cylinder locks. The "wings" are used for double wafer locks to place the pick between them while picking. You may bend these wings slightly if you wish for better accessibility to the tumblers. If you do so, you must place the body of the Dragon in a vise and heat the wings for three minutes with a 1500-watt hair dryer. Slowly and carefully, bend both prongs at the same time with a pair of pliers. Remember to bend only to about 15 or 20 degrees; if you bend them any further, you might break off a prong.

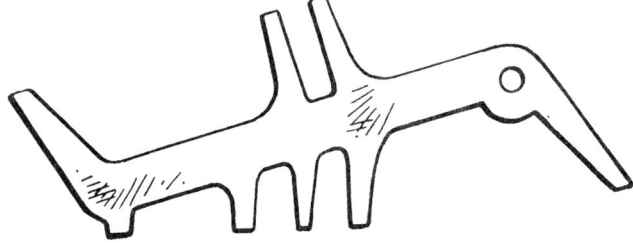

Figure 11. Universal tension wrench called the "Dragon."

In order to make this tool, you will need .035-inch stainless steel stock. The piece should be 3 1/2 inches by 1 1/4 inches. Make your pattern as described on pages 9 and 10. When you have a painted pattern on your stock, rough cut it out with your cutoff wheel. You will have to use the cutoff wheel to get between the Dragon's legs and wings, so cut carefully in these places. The only way you will be able to finish these places is with the cutoff. The rest of the areas can be cut so that you have just a little metal to grind. Now replace your cutoff wheel with the burnishing wheel and smooth all sharp edges. Be sure to leave relatively sharp right angles on the Dragon's feet since they have to be able to grab rim

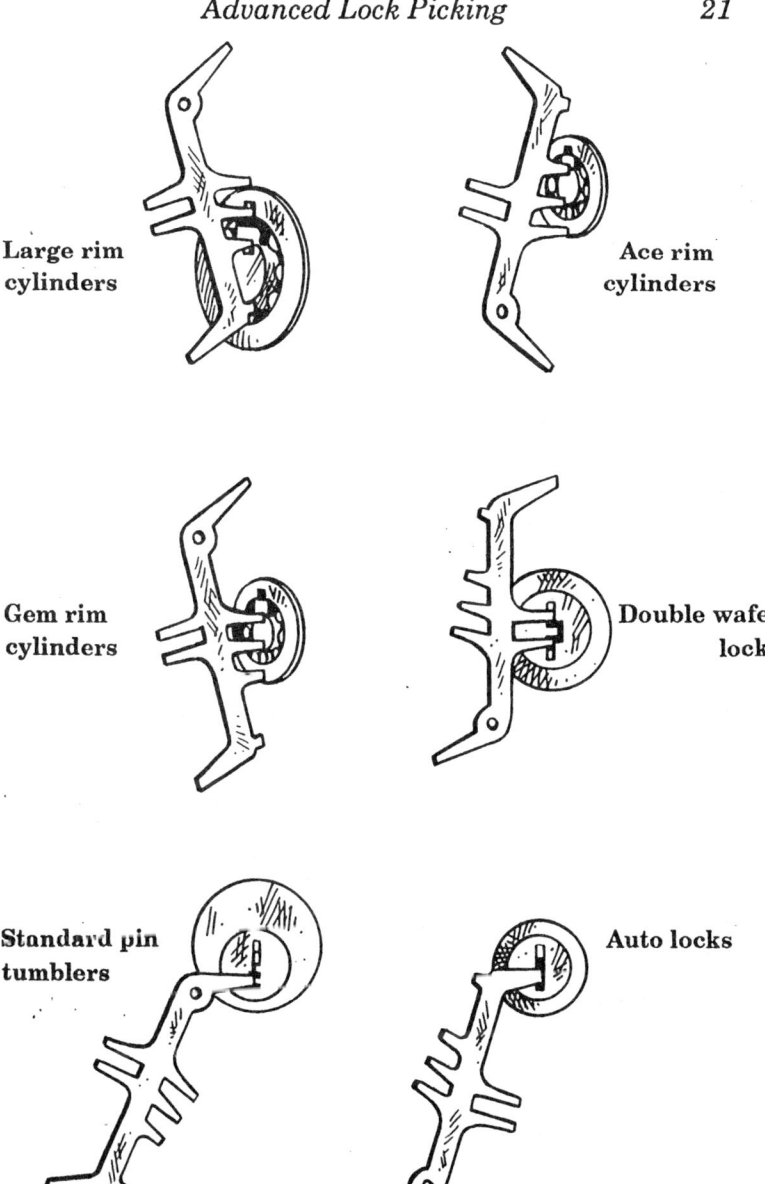

Large rim
cylinders

Ace rim
cylinders

Gem rim
cylinders

Double wafer
locks

Standard pin
tumblers

Auto locks

Figure 12. Using the Dragon universal tension wrench.

cylinders. The front of the first leg and the back of the last leg can be smoothed with your burnisher to keep the tool user-friendly; otherwise, it could snag clothing or your wallet.

The key chain hole is optional but may be drilled on a drill press since stainless is so hard. Start with a small drill bit to make a pilot hole, than finish it with a 1/8-inch bit. You may also want to chamfer the hole by hand with a 1/4-inch drill bit when you are done.

Making this tool is not as difficult as it may first appear. The hardest part is cutting out the paper pattern. The time it takes to make is well worth it, since nothing like it exists on the market. I am the sole patent owner and have given you permission to make it for your own use.

Figure 13 illustrates a pattern for a pick I call the "Serpent," which has a diamond tip pick on one end and a ball pick on the other. The diamond tip is obviously useful for pin and wafer tumbler locks, and the ball end is used exclusively on double wafer locks. If you wish, you can make the central 3/4 inch of the shank wider for easier handling. My hands are large, yet I find the size illustrated suits me fine. If you learned to pick tumbler locks with a safety pin, as I did, you'll find that this size will work well—you'll have less metal to carry.

diamond · ball

Figure 13. Serpent pick.

With the Serpent and the Dragon, one can open a wide variety of locks. With practice on each aspect of the tools, one basically becomes a walking key.

Warded-Lever Locks

Figure 14 shows a few warded-lever lock pick keys. Examples A and B are skeleton keys made from .045-inch stock. They are used on the old-style door locks of years past and, surprisingly, are still in use in isolated cases. Some old office buildings and homes still have them on the doors. These two tools are designed with maximum clearance while maintaining enough metal to keep them strong.

The pick key in example C is made from .025-inch stock and is used on old desks and cabinets. It is made thin so it will bypass the center restricting post on these types of locks. Examples D and E are pick keys made from about .035-inch stock. They are used on simple courtesy dispensing devices in public places, such as the paper towel box in bathrooms, and so on.

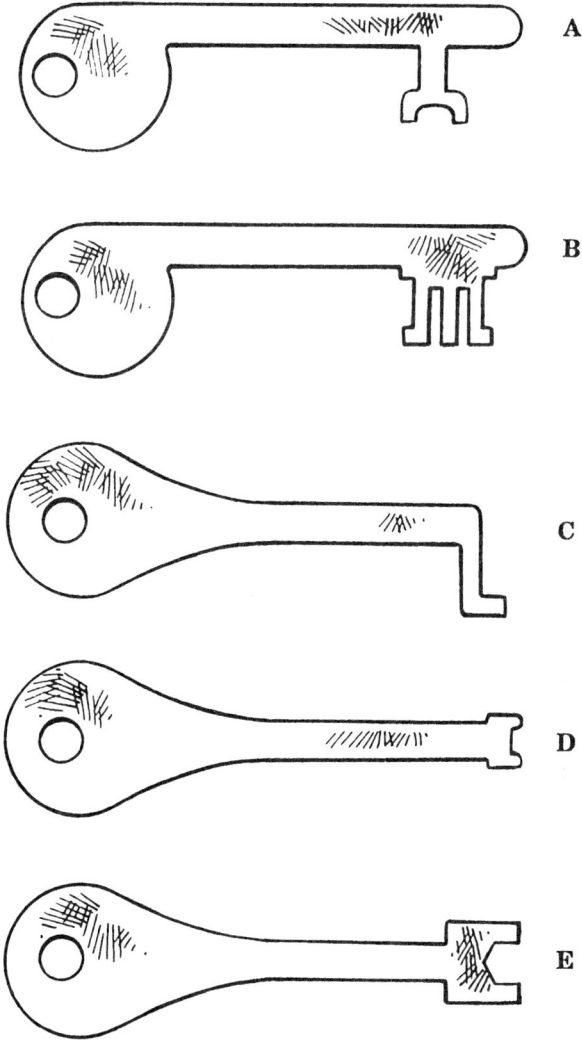

Figure 14. Five keys for warded-lever locks.

Magnetic Locks

Magnetic locks are usually divided into two groups. The purely magnetic ones are basically mechanical in nature. These operate on the principle that like poles repel. The other group of magnetic locks uses electronic sensors to read the small magnetic fields embedded into plastic cards. These fields are detected and decoded to determine whether or not to allow entry.

The mechanical-type magnetic lock has magnets super-glued onto a spring-loaded cam network. These magnets are arranged in such a way that the key's magnets will repel the magnet-operated cam through the bolt, thus opening the lock.

Although magnetic locks were discussed in my previous book, there seemed to be some questions from my readers about the magnetic pick. Most of you were wondering if it could be made portable, and in this chapter we will discuss three portable magnetic lock picks. The first one is rather simple and works 75 percent of the time. The second one is much more complex, and you may need a friend who is an electronics technician to build it for you. Since locks are going the way of electronic technology these days, a knowledge of electronics is useful to the master lock picker.

These picks are used in a stroking fashion, either in and out through the key slot of a magnetic card lock or across the side of a magnetic padlock. The basic principle is to get the magnetic domains in the lock to vibrate, allowing you to catch the bolt at the right moment to open it (see Figure 15).

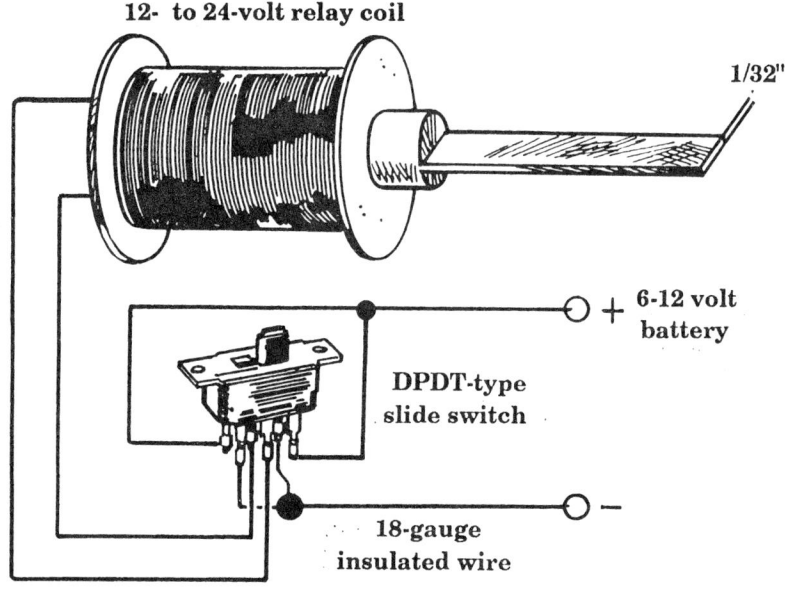

Figure 15. Magnetic "key" mechanism.

In order to do this, a quickly changing magnetic field is generated by a coil of insulated magnet wire and a source of electrical power. In Figure 15, a battery pack (four to eight D cells) is the power source. The switch is rapidly flipped back and forth to cause the current through the coil to flow one way, then the other. This causes the magnetic field to first go north, then south, then north, and so on. The coil can be salvaged from an old 12- to 24-volt solenoid, or you may choose to buy a new one. The important thing is that you need to remove the core (iron slug) from the solenoid, find its diameter, and get a steel rod the same diameter—about 4 inches long. Carefully grind down 2 inches (half the rod length) until it is about 1/32 inch thick so that it will fit into most magnetic card locks. After that, epoxy the unground side of the slug into the coil. This is your portable electromagnetic pick.

Be sure to add an on/off switch from the battery pack since the DPDT slide switch acts only as an oscillator switch and doesn't turn the unit off. This unit may cause television and radio interference.

Figure 16 is a more sophisticated version that oscillates the electromagnetic field for you. It is quiet and can be made small enough to fit in your shirt pocket. You will still be using a battery pack (two 9-volt transistor batteries, to be exact), but the unit frees up one of your hands while in operation. It is basically a multivibrator circuit, generating a square wave pulse, like a low voltage AC source. DC current comes from the batteries and this circuit converts it to AC for the pick. If you know some basic electronics, you'll find that it is easy to build. If not, have a friend who is familiar with the subject build it for you. You can use the same solenoid coil-type pick with this circuit and both picks are safe to operate. Make sure you use electrical tape to insulate all exposed connections. Also, don't leave the units on when not in use or you'll run your batteries down.

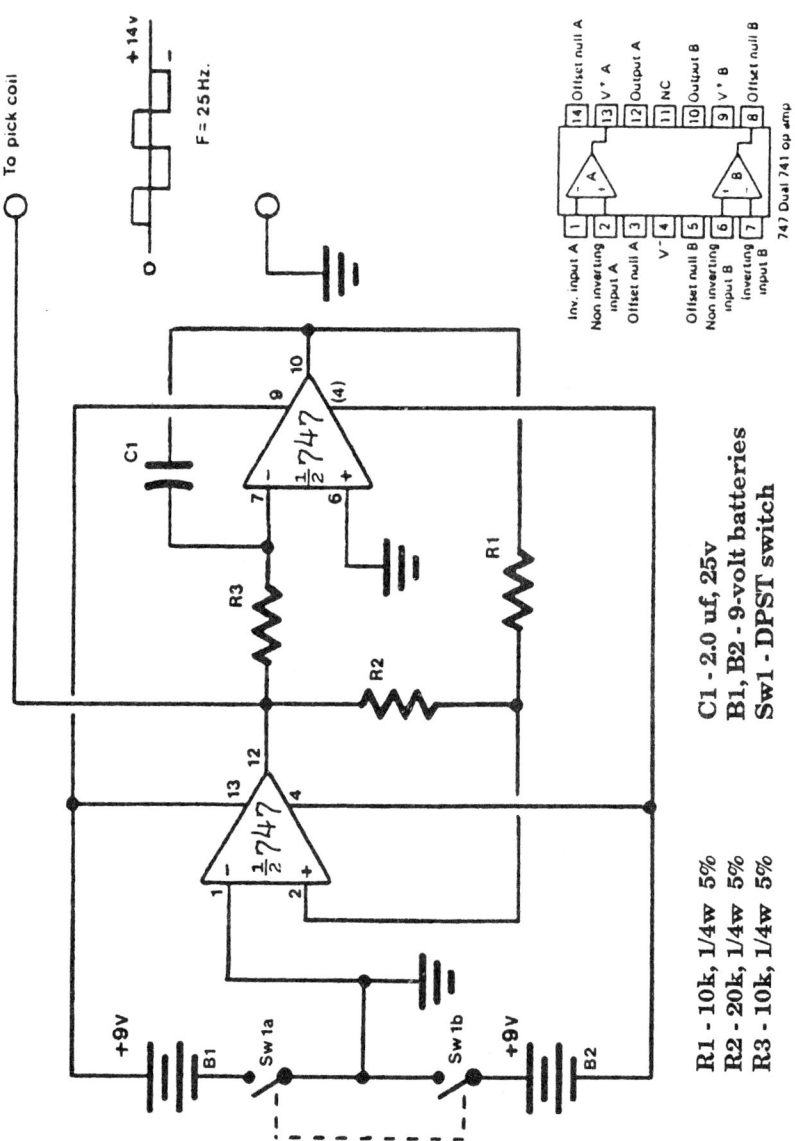

C1 - 2.0 uf, 25v
B1, B2 - 9-volt batteries
Sw1 - DPST switch

R1 - 10k, 1/4w 5%
R2 - 20k, 1/4w 5%
R3 - 10k, 1/4w 5%

Figure 16. Magnetic lock pick schematic.

Magnetic Card Locks

Some magnetic locks use microprocessing electronic circuits to control entry. They are in current use on hotel doors and at the workplace. Though formidable in appearance, they have inherent weaknesses. Before we discuss "picking" these types of locks, let's see how they work.

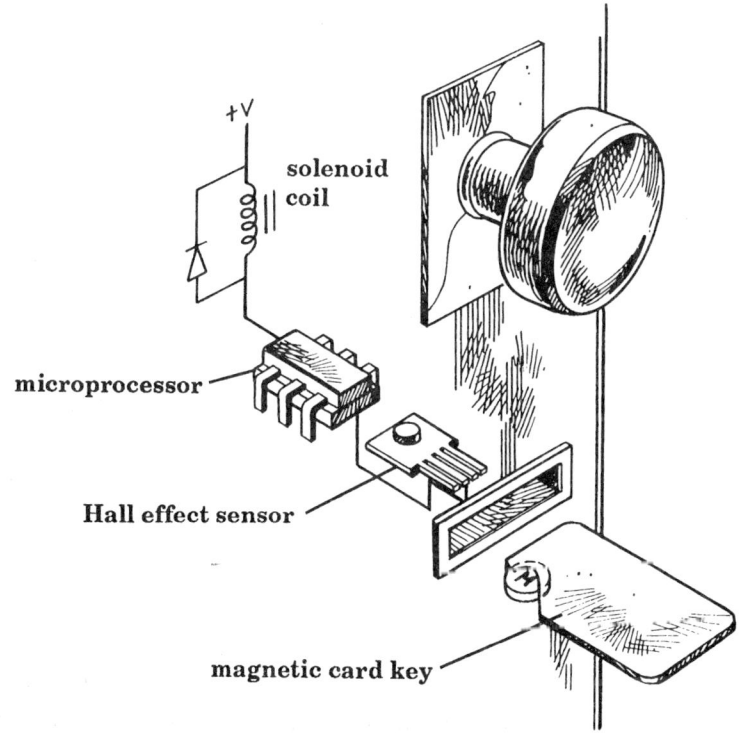

Figure 17. Magnetic card lock.

A linear output transducer (a Hall effect sensor) picks up a magnetic field from the card. There are dozens of sensors in the cardway and each one responds to a magnetic field from the magnets molded into the card. When the Hall effect sensor determines the polarity (north or south) of a particular field, it sends a signal to the microprocessor. This information is either go or no-go. When all of the sensors are sending go signals, the microprocessor determines whether or not they are all go and if they are at the right frequency. On some locks, the sensors are "gated" to allow only one narrow band of oscillating signals at so many cycles per second. These cards have their own power supply (battery) and actually pulse their magnetic fields. With all signals at go status, the microprocessor sends a pulse to the electromagnetic solenoid latch, thus allowing the door to be opened.

Some systems use a constant speed motor-driven tray to slide the multicoded card past the sensors to read it, and then spit it back out to you. In order to effectively open this type of magnetic card lock, we'll need to use strong magnetic fields so as to not get the magnetic pick too deeply into the cardway. We will also need to generate a continually changing magnetic field with multiple frequencies.

Magnetic Card Pick

If you have already built the portable magnetic pick, you have the electromagnetic pick assembly on hand. This will be the device that will put out the kind of electromagnetic fields we will need. To generate these fields, we will have to use a circuit that is a little more complex than the previous magnetic pick.

The circuit illustrated in Figure 18 is a schematic of

a random noise generator. When completed, it can fit into a matchbox (approximately 1 inch by 1 1/2 inches by 1/2 inch). It is basically a noisy amplifier that has high gain and a low impedance output which produces a large signal noise, enough so that it will drive a 24-volt solenoid coil and produce a continual oscillating magnetic field with random frequencies rich in harmonics.

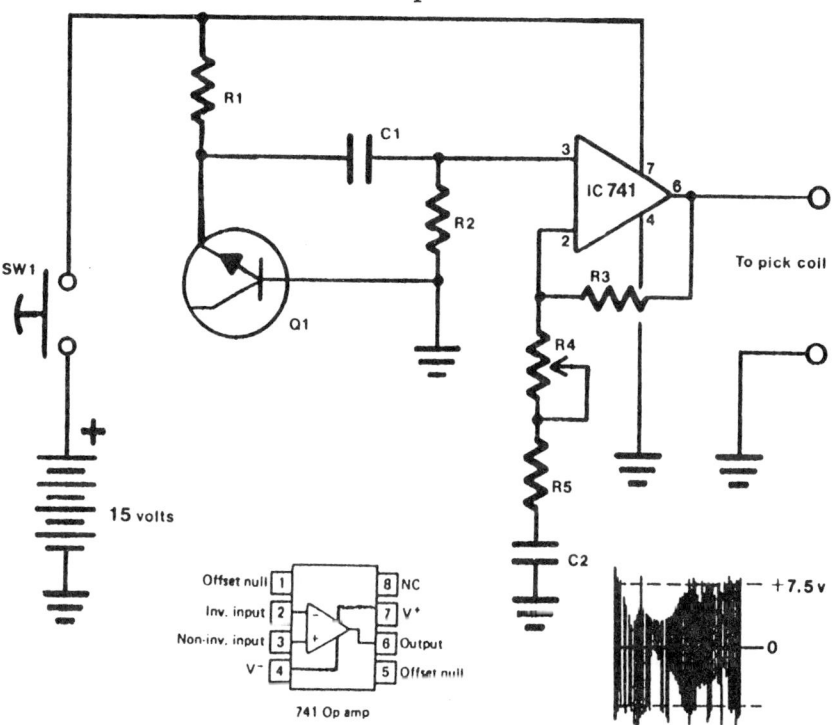

R1 - 220k, 1/4w 5%	R5 - 10k, 1/4w 5%
R2 - 1.0M, 1/4w 5%	C1 - .01 uf
R3 - 1.0M, 1/4w 5%	C2 - .1 uf
R4 - 100k, linear taper	Q1 - any NPN transistor

Figure 18. Magnetic card pick schematic.

This type of signal is caused by the zener breakdown of the transistor junction in Q1. The signal is then amplified by the operational amplifier IC 74I, generating electromagnetic fields in the pick coil. The battery pack is simply ten size AA, 1.5-volt batteries taped and soldered in series, with short pieces of insulated wire, positive to negative. SW 1 is a momentary push-button switch designed to pulse the fields into the Hall effect sensors if stroking them won't work. Potentiometer R4 controls the intensity of the fields. On locks that do not have a motor-driven tray, set the intensity at one-half to three-quarters of full power to avoid overtaxing the sensors. On motor-driven tray-type magnetic card locks, go full blast to keep from getting your pick stuck in the cardway; just place it about 1/4 inch into the entrance of the cardway, and it should open.

When you use this device, the continually changing magnetic fields stimulate the Hall effect sensors with a flurry of information. In turn, the sensors determine that somewhere in that message was its coded frequency with its proper polarity. This in turn signals the microprocessor that something is happening, which finds the proper code out of all that noise and activates the solenoid latch. The latch can be heard as a loud clack when its driving solenoid fires.

If you are not familiar with building electronic circuits, have a friend build it for you. The total cost of the parts is around five dollars. The batteries are the major expense, but they should last for about twenty-four hours of continual use and longer with intermittent use. Be sure to use an eight-pin, dual inline socket for IC 741 for easy replacement. The other components should never go bad.

Disc Tumbler
and Puzzle Locks

Some residential and business doors use puzzle locks that have five numbers that must be pressed in sequence to open the door. These are sometimes referred to as push-button locks. Simplex Security Company makes a good mechanism, and since it is typical of most of these types of locks, we will use one as an example.

One technique used to open such a lock is to apply rotational pressure on the knob and push each button, seeing which one offers the most resistance. This is usually the first combination number. Release the knob, push the first number you found, and apply rotational pressure again. Now search for the second number like you did the first one. Release the knob again, and apply rotational pressure again. Find the third number the same way, and continue on until the lock opens. You must release the knob each time you find a likely number and start the process over to find the next one.

You should be able to open the lock within five minutes. If not, I have had limited success in randomly,

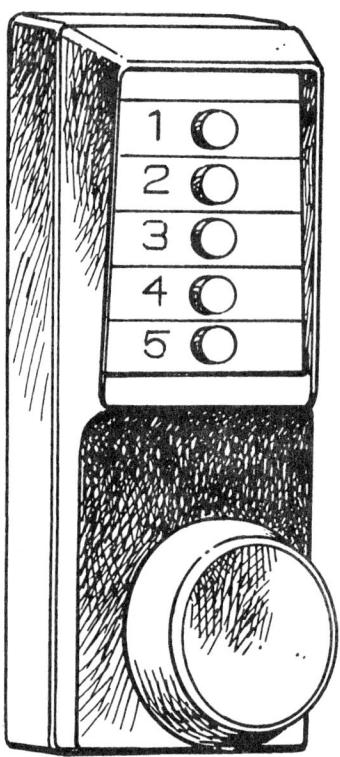

Figure 19. Push-button puzzle lock.

and very quickly, pushing out the numbers until you find the proper combination. The trouble with this method is that you seldom catch what the combination was and have to go through the whole process again in order to gain access a second time. As usual, practice will shorten the time it takes you to open these locks.

Some of my readers have been having trouble opening Sesame-type padlocks. These locks have isolated bolts; that is, they cannot be manipulated open by touch and listen exclusively. If you ever have to open one in a hurry, I suggest the following method.

Figure 20 shows three-wheel and four-wheel model Sesame locks that have been drilled. For illustration purposes, I have drilled the holes larger than necessary. Through the holes you can see the cams rotate as you turn the wheels. Simply rotate each wheel to line up the flat spot on the cams so that they are straight across as you look into the holes.

The numbers at which the wheels are now set do not comprise the actual combinations. However, adding seven to each number on the dials will give you the right combination. For example, after all of the cams are lined up straight across and the wheels are set at 1-3-8, as shown in the top illustration on the following page, simply add seven to each one to get the combination of 8-0-5.

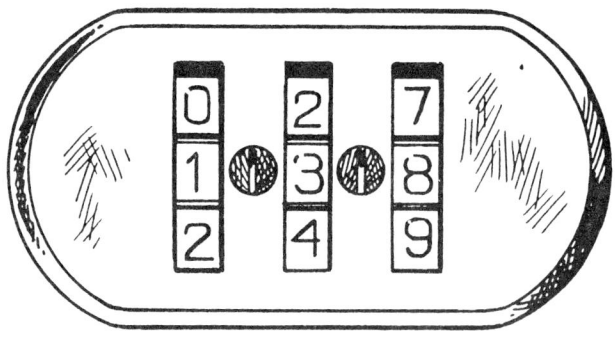

1-3-8 = 8-0-5 to open

8-1-6-5 = 5-8-3-2 to open

Figure 20. Three- and four-wheel Sesame locks.

Energizing Your Hands

I would like to introduce an old kung-fu method used to strengthen and add flexibility to your fingers and hands. In kung-fu, the hands are regarded as terminal points for *chi,* or life force. I don't want to sound mystical, but there is great power of spirit in most schools of kung-fu. Your fingers and hands can become clear open channels for your mind's intentions. I do this exercise to open these channels and you can do it too.

The first part of this exercise is called Energizing Hands. The hands are energy gateways to and from your body. They allow energy to flow because they are termination points from your heart *chakra,* or center, where life force resides. In other words, your fingers are the receptors and transmitters of energy. The forearms are the storehouse for this energy and by stretching your forearms in a certain way, you can induce large amounts of chi energy into your hands and fingertips.

First, sit on the floor cross-legged on a thin cushion. Try to get comfortable while keeping your back relaxed and straight. Cross-legged is best because the back is straighter and excess energy that might otherwise escape from your feet goes back into your body. Indian style is OK. If you can get into a half- or full-lotus position, that's even better. The main point is to be erect and relaxed with your eyes open. Drop your shoulders, and let your arms hang to your sides with your palms flat to the floor. Loosen up your arms; try to imagine them being pulled down because of the tremendous weight of your hands. Keep your shoulders back and down.

Now, lift your hands up from the floor about half an inch without moving your shoulders up. Your hands should be parallel to the floor but not touching it. With your hands in this position, you can reap huge amounts of energy from Mother Earth. S t r e t c h the arms down—make it almost hurt. Stay in this position five to ten minutes, or as long as possible. You will start to shake all over after a few minutes. Don't be concerned. You are collecting power from the Earth. The longer you hold this position, the more energy your hands and forearms will accumulate.

At some point you will feel the energy entering your heart chakra to store itself there. This energy will stay there until you need to use it for "fight or flight" situations (or for picking locks). In fact, you could charge yourself up in this manner whenever you encounter a stressful or otherwise difficult situation. This is a very powerful technique. It is used in Tibetan kung-fu to subdue the opponent.

You can locate missing or lost people after you have practiced this for a while by holding your hand (left if you are right-handed, right if you are left-handed) up to the general direction of their disappearance. When you feel a warm buzzing sensation in your fingertips, chances are they will be in that area. You can also detect intruders in this way. Your hands can be powerful guides when you need them.

Remember to keep the palms flat and fingers together when doing this exercise. Make sure that your thumbs are not hanging out and keep your shoulders *down*. Make it hurt. Don't hurt yourself by being overly zealous, but make the arms and shoulders *stretch*.

Your palms should be hot by now—they will be charged with chi. If you were to look at them, you would see that they are red with white specks in them. The white specks are areas of intense energy radiation. A Kirlian photograph made with special equipment would detect this as brilliant lights shooting out from your hands. The hand that you are now looking at can shatter a brick! That is how much energy you can muster in such a short time. But *please,* don't try shattering bricks because other techniques are involved to do that safely; you could hurt yourself.

Practice this exercise five minutes a day for a few weeks and you will definitely notice an improvement in your lock picking abilities.

The second part of this exercise can be practiced anywhere and as many times as you like. It is called "Disbursement," or the outward flow of accumulated energy. This is done by popping your finger joints in an extended stretching motion. After you have energized your hands, slowly lift your arms up in front of you and really stretch your fingers as if each one were extending out and out. This is a safe and proven way to pop your knuckles to make your hands and fingers strong and flexible. Kung-fu students and teachers have been doing it for centuries and none of them ended up with arthritis or anything like it. Your fingers may not pop at first, but with practice, more and more of your finger joints will loosen up.

While doing this you should try to imagine that beams of light are shooting out from the tips of your fingers. You can do this exercise standing, sitting, or lying down, although I recommend you do it in conjunction with the energizing exercise for a few weeks until your hands have loosened up.

Now, slowly close your hands in a clawlike manner, closing one set of joints at a time. It should take you about ten seconds to get them closed. Keep your fingers stiff to cause tension in them while closing. Your joints will really start to pop, and when you are done, they will feel quite pliable and strong. At this point the exercise is over and you may find picking locks a little easier and faster.

Tips for Success

Due to limited time and space, as well as individual styles of learning, I am unable to cover all of the locks used today. Therefore, I encourage the sincere novice to purchase locks of interest and disassemble them to learn how they operate. Then you will be able to figure out a way to open them. The biggest deterrent to lock picking is the lack of knowledge of a lock's inner functions. With this in mind, you will find that opening locks is just a matter of discovery.

In the art of lock picking, as with any fine art, nothing compares with experience through practice. A simple way for you to get that experience is to practice with tumbler padlocks. They are small, portable sources of working material for your experience. Start a collection and pick them while you are watching television or just loafing around the house. The greater the variety of locks you have, the wider your range of experience will become and locks will not become obstacles to your goals.

One of the most amazing things I have discovered in past years is that many people I have taught to pick locks are not what you would call very mechanically inclined. Yet, curiosity on their part has led them to become virtually master lock pickers. This tickles me to no end.

It is also important to remember that making your own tools will let you have access to a much larger range of locks, mostly because your tools are *yours*. You made them and they work. There is a powerful psychological factor involved here. Your first few sets may not be exactly what you want, but you will probably wear them out anyway through practice. By the time you make your third set, they will be perfect because you will know how you want them to work.

Practice picking with thin cotton or wool gloves. I wear thin wool gloves in winter because they are durable and keep your hands warm even when wet. Some locks require more time to pick in cold weather because they have a tendency to stick from moisture frozen inside the lock. You must keep your fingers and hands warm in order to successfully open them. I have never been able to pick open a lock with cold hands.

I first learned how to pick locks by taking them apart to see how they worked. At some point in my young career, I had made a "Lock Box"—a wooden box covered with mounted locks. It looked ridiculous—seventy locks on a box with cheap hinges. There were padlocks dangling off the sides, safe locks protruding out the back, and almost every kind of lock imaginable on the top. The inside contained spare lock parts and various tools. I would practice every night picking all of them. My friends thought I was nuts—until they saw me in action. Then, of course, they wanted to learn too.

Most locksmith shops will sell you old discarded locks of all kinds for the price of brass by weight. You can probably pick up a hundred locks with all the associated hardware (trimmings) for about $10 to $15. If you are at the right place at the right time, you can get some old safe locks, which are great fun to play with. The only tools you will really need are a pair of pliers, vise grips, a crescent wrench, various screwdrivers (both standard and Phillips), some files (round, flat, and square), and a drill with a set of bits and hole saws.

You can make the box out of pine or oak if you wish. With a varnished finish and polished brass locks, it can be a rather attractive novelty in your home. Don't use brass polish on the locks, as the residue will get into the tumblers and cylinders and cause problems. Use an old toothbrush and toothpaste to clean up the face of the locks. Rinse with hot water and dry them by a furnace duct or in the sun.

Building yourself a Lock Box will make the art of lock picking more fun and give you a lot of experience.